Dropshipping E-commerce Business Model 2019

$10,000/month Ultimate Guide - Make a Passive Income Fortune with Shopify, Amazon FBA, Affiliate marketing, Retail Arbitrage, Ebay and Social Media

By

Steven Sparrow

Table of Contents

Introduction 5

Chapter 1: Understanding How Dropshipping Works 10

Chapter 2: The Benefits of Working in Dropshipping 16
- Little Investment to Start 16
- Easy to Get Started 18
- Little to No Overhead Costs.. 19
- Lots of Products to Choose From 20
- A Global Market... 21
- Easy to Scale Later on If You Want 22
- Easy to Automate 23

Chapter 3: The Drawbacks of Dropshipping 25
- Sudden Shortages in Stock 25
- Customer Service is All on You....................................... 27
- Less Control Over Your Own Business 27
- Potential Issues with Quality Control............................. 29
- Hard to Find Products That Will Make Enough Money 30
- Supplier Errors 31

Chapter 4: How to Get Started with Your Dropshipping Business..34
- How to Choose Your Dropshipping Niche 34
- Find a Supplier... 38
- Get Your Sales Tax ID 39
- Pick Out Your Products 41

Choose Your Selling Platform 42
Setting Up a Strategy to Bring Customers in 43
Picking the Right Price 49

Chapter 5: How to Pick a Supplier and How to Pick Out a Product 52

How to Pick Out a Good Supplier 52
How to Pick Out the Right Products to Sell 55

Chapter 6: How to Handle Your Customers and Provide Exemplary Customer Service 61

You are the One Responsible 62
Understand Your Customers 63
Know About Your Products 64
Happiness is the Top Priority 65
How to Set Yourself Apart from the Competition 67

Chapter 7: How to Handle Security Issues With Your Business 73

Select a Platform that is Secure 73
Set Higher Standards for Passwords 74
Protect Against Any DoS Attacks 75
Use an SSL Protection Layer 76

Chapter 8: How to Scale Your Business 79

Add More Products to Your Inventory 80
Consider Seasonal Items 81
Hire Others to Help You Manage the Business 82

Chapter 9: How to Dropship with Shopify 85

Chapter 10: How to Dropship On Amazon and eBay 92

Dropshipping on Amazon 92

Dropshipping on eBay 97

Chapter 11: Creating a Personal Website for Your Dropshipping Business 101

Get Your Domain Name and Web Hosting 102

Install WordPress 104

Set Up the Website and Pick the Right Plugins 107

Chapter 12: Do I Need to Use Social Media for My Business? 110

Chapter 13: What About Using Affiliate Marketing? 117

Chapter 14: How Amazon FBA Can Help You Grow Your Business 124

Amazon FBA 125

Chapter 15: Tips to Make Your Dropshipping Business As Successful As Possible 134

Focus on the Marketing 134

Do Not Underprice the Products 136

Pick a Product That Makes a Good Profit Margin 137

Find Ways to Bundle Items Together 139

Pick the Right Platform That You Like the Best 140

Always Provide the Best Customer Service 141

Order the Product Yourself Before Selling it 142

Conclusion 145

© **Copyright 2019 by __Steven Sparrow____ - All rights reserved.**

The following book is reproduced below with the goal of providing information that is as accurate and reliable as possible. Regardless, purchasing this book can be seen as consent to the fact that both the publisher and the author of this book are in no way experts on the topics discussed within and that any recommendations or suggestions that are made herein are for entertainment purposes only. Professionals should be consulted as needed prior to undertaking any of the action endorsed herein.

This declaration is deemed fair and valid by both the American Bar Association and the Committee of Publishers Association and is legally binding throughout the United States.

Furthermore, the transmission, duplication, or reproduction of any of the following work including specific information will be considered an illegal act irrespective of if it is done electronically or in print. This extends to creating a secondary or tertiary copy of the work or a recorded copy and is only allowed with the express written consent from the Publisher. All additional rights reserved.

The information in the following pages is broadly considered a truthful and accurate account of facts and as such, any inattention, use, or misuse of the information in question by the reader will render any resulting actions solely under their purview. There are no scenarios in which the publisher or the original author of this work can be in any fashion deemed liable for any hardship or damages that may befall them after undertaking information described herein.

Additionally, the information in the following pages is intended only for informational purposes and should thus be thought of as universal. As befitting its nature, it is presented without assurance regarding its prolonged validity or interim quality. Trademarks that are mentioned are done without written consent and can in no way be considered an endorsement from the trademark holder.

Introduction

Congratulations on downloading *Dropshipping E-commerce Business Model 2019* and thank you for doing so.

The following chapters will discuss everything that you need to know in order to get started with your own dropshipping business. There are a lot of different types of businesses that you can choose to work with. Many of them claim to be part-time and can offer you a lot of money on the side but most of them end up failing, taking up too much time, and not providing you with the money that was promised.

Dropshipping is a process that is different from these other options. With this method, you get the benefit of working the hours that are best for you. If you want to just work a few hours a week, you simply have to just sell a few products at a time to keep the time management easy. If you want to turn this into a full-time income, you simply scale the business up and start selling more products and advertising more. There really isn't any other business model that works as successfully as working with dropshipping.

This guidebook is going to take some time to look at all the information that you need to know in order to get started with dropshipping. We will take a look at what dropshipping is, some of the advantages of working with dropshipping, how to choose a good supplier and a good product to work with, and more just to get things started.

Inside, we will also have a discussion about which platforms are the best for helping you to see results with your selling. You can choose to create your personal website and sell the products through that method, or you can work through some other popular websites such as Shopify, Amazon, or eBay to sell your products.

In addition, we will spend time looking at all the other parts of dropshipping that you need to know to get the most out of this business and get it to work for you. We will look at how to keep your website safe so customers trust you with their payments, how to work with social media to grow your website, how to provide the best customer service each time and even some methods on how you can beat out the competition and get ahead.

While there are many other business opportunities out there that you can choose to work with, none are going to be as successful and as easy to start as dropshipping. While you will need to put in a little bit of work to get this started, you will find that compared to some of the other methods of making money from home, this is one of the best. When you are ready to get started with your own dropshipping business, make sure to read through this guidebook to learn how!

There are plenty of books on this subject on the market, so thanks again for choosing this one! Every effort was made to ensure it is full of as much useful information as possible. Please enjoy!

Chapter 1: Understanding How Dropshipping Works

Before we can get into some of the steps on how to start your own dropshipping business, it is important to have a good understanding of what this process is all about. Dropshipping is basically a business model where a company or an individual is able to do all of their operations without having to own a warehouse to store the products, without having to maintain inventory, and they don't even need to ship out the products to the customers.

The way that this process works is that the retailer is going to partner up with a supplier. This supplier will either warehouse or manufacture various products for the retailer to choose from. The supplier will then pack the product and ship directly to the customer once they received an order from the retailer (which is you in this supply chain). The supplier is doing this on your behalf during this process.

To break this down a bit further, here are some of the steps that explain better how dropshipping works:

1. The customer is going to go to an online store for a retailer and then places an order for a product that is there.
2. The retailer, either manually or automatically, forwards the order, as well as the details about the customer over to the supplier.
3. The supplier will then pack the order and ship it out to the customer. The package will have the name of the retailer to help maintain the business image of the dropshipper.

This kind of business model has gotten a lot of popularity in recent years because it has helped to eliminate the need for a store owner to be in a physical location such as in their own office space or warehouse. Anyone can join this business model as long as they have an internet connection and a laptop.

Typically, the profit margin for a dropshipping business will be somewhere between 15 and 45 percent. However, depending on the product, it is possible that the amount could be higher, sometimes up to 100 percent. How do you determine how viable this option is and how much you are going to make?

This is often going to do more with finding the right niche and a good supplier so that you can enter into a market that has good demand but isn't overly saturated already. The more saturated the market is, the harder it is going to be for you to find your voice there. As an effect, your margins and your sales are going to be much lower.

A good way to help you to get higher margins is to try and source right from the manufacturer directly rather than going through a supplier or a vendor. This is a bit harder to do, but if you can accomplish it, this effectively cuts out the middleman in the scenario and can save you some money in the process.

Once you have been able to get your dropshipping business off the ground and gain a bit of traction in the market, you will find that this kind of business can quickly start being a money-making machine, one that only needs a little bit of input. It does take some time and some work, and you won't be able to get it done within a few weeks. You have to be willing to put in a lot of work. But if you are good at finding reputable suppliers, good at finding products that will sell well and earn you a higher margin, you can become successful in this kind of business as well.

Who Can Dropshipping Be Good For?

There are a lot of people who can benefit from starting their own dropshipping business. Anyone who wants to earn a side income to help pay the bills and who can devote at least a little bit of time each day to this endeavor would do well at dropshipping. Anyone who wants to get started with growing their business but who doesn't have a lot of capital to spend from the beginning can benefit from his business model. Anyone who wants to be able to stay at home and pursue things other than their traditional job will benefit from this type of business model, too.

There are a few different types of entrepreneurs who will really benefit from the idea of dropshipping. Some of these include:

- Validating Entrepreneur: This business model can be a good way for the individual to test out a new product or a new startup before they invest a lot of money into inventory they are worried may not sell.

- Budget Entrepreneur: Dropshipping is a very inexpensive method of selling online because you are not responsible for purchasing any inventory upfront. This can work out as a great business model for those individuals who want to start a business but want to keep their startup costs low or who are on a limited budget.

- The First Time Entrepreneur: This model of business is a great option for someone who is just starting out with the idea of selling online. Selling online isn't something that everyone finds easy. Driving traffic to your website and then converting that traffic can take a lot of time for a new marketer. Because dropshipping is low in cost, it can allow a new entrepreneur some time to learn how to set up a store, drive traffic, and optimize conversions before they invest more money into their own business.

- Walmart Entrepreneur: This type of business can also be good for someone who would like a chance to sell a ton of models and products. Depending on how much each item costs and how big you want to grow, acquiring all of this inventory for a traditional business can be really expensive. But with dropshipping, this is possible without spending a lot of money.

As you can see, there are many benefits that come with working in dropshipping. Many different individuals will find this as a great option to starting their own business, whether they are doing it as a method to help them to see if this is right for them before starting their own business, if they are using it as a part-time income, or if they are using it to make a full-time income on their time. Dropshipping can be a great business model for anyone who is willing to put in the time and the work.

Chapter 2: The Benefits of Working in Dropshipping

There are a lot of different business opportunities out there that you can choose to go with. However, none of them provide the same benefits that you can get from starting your own dropshipping business. This kind of business doesn't require a lot of money to start, can take just a few steps to get it up and running, introduces you to a global market right from the start, and so much more. Let's take a look at some of the benefits of working with your own dropshipping business and why you should consider starting yours today.

Little Investment to Start

Starting your own dropshipping business requires very little investment to get going. You don't have to pay to make the products, you don't have to keep an inventory for the products, and you do not have to hire a team to help you run the business or even to pay for shipping. In fact, it is possible to get started with drop shipping without paying for anything upfront.

If you choose to sell the products from your own website (and there are some benefits to that), you will have to pay a bit to get the website up and running. If you decide to go with Amazon or eBay, you can get the item listed and then you will pay once the item actually sells. If you plan to use a bit of advertising to draw more interest to your items, then you will need to pay for that as well.

As a dropshipper, it is really in your control how much you would like to spend to get started. Some people are able to start this kind of business for nothing, and others like to spend a bit to help set themselves apart from other sellers. The great thing about this business is that you get to be the one who decides all of it and you can keep the costs as low as you need.

Easy to Get Started

While we will discuss this in a bit more detail later, it is pretty easy to get started with your own dropshipping business. Unlike some other business models, you will find that this business can be started relatively quickly. Keep in mind that you do need to do a bit of research on suppliers and products. It is important that you don't rush in and pick the first product you see. But comparatively, you can't find an easier type of business.

With dropshipping, you simply need to find a niche to work in, find a product and the right supplier of that product to fill that niche, list it in some manner online (such as on Amazon or your own website), and then wait for a customer order. Once the customer orders, you will take what they pay you and place an order directly with the suppliers. The supplier will then send the item out to the customer, and you will end up with a happy customer.

Of course, there are times when things won't work out exactly as you had planned, but there are steps you can take to limit issues and keep things going smoothly. Those basic steps above are really all you need to get started with this kind of business model.

Little to No Overhead Costs

As a dropshipper, you will have limited to no overhead costs. You are not required to keep any of the products on hand or to have an inventory of any kind at all. With this business model, you simply list the products that you want to sell somewhere online such as on Amazon or eBay. Then, when a customer orders, you will use that money to place an order directly with the supplier. The supplier sends the item directly to the customer, not to you. You don't have to worry about keeping all of the products on hand for each customer, which means there is very little cost for you.

There are a few costs that come with dropshipping but you do have some control over them. For example, if you use your own website, you may have to put a bit of money into that. There are usually a few fees associated with listing on eBay and Amazon as well. If you wish to advertise on social media, you will also need to pay a little bit. But as a business owner, you can choose how much you would like to spend on the products. And despite the other expenses, there will never be an overhead cost for running your business.

Lots of Products to Choose From

When it comes to dropshipping, you will find that there are a ton of products that you can sell for your business. There are hundreds of suppliers and each of them can offer you something unique to work with. This means that it is easier for you to reach your own niche because there is sure to be a product out there that will work for you.

Make sure that you take the time to really look through a bunch of suppliers and the products that they offer. You want to make sure that you find a good supplier, a unique product, and something that is in high demand but is still not getting reached well by other sellers. If you can combine all of these together, you will find that it is easier to get more sales on your site.

A Global Market

Since dropshipping and all of the business you do with it will occur online, you get the opportunity to work with a global market, even as a beginner. With a traditional business, you will have to start out by working in your local community. After some time has passed and you see a good amount of profits and interest, you may decide to expand out into your area, then the state, and then the country. Eventually, you may decide to reach out to a global market, but that is only if your business gets that far. Many businesses are happy to just expand a little bit in their region.

But with dropshipping, you can make your products available to a large market right from the beginning. If you list on sites like eBay, Amazon, and Shopify, or even if you do your own website, you are already reaching a potential global market. This is huge. That means more people who may potentially be interested in your product, and more potential to grow your own dropshipping business in no time.

Easy to Scale Later on If You Want

When you first get started with this kind of business, you want to keep it simple. You may only want to start out with a few products to keep it simple and learn the ropes, and that is just fine. But over time, as you start to get the hang of dropshipping and everything that goes along with it. You can then decide to scale your business and make it bigger later on.

That is part of the beauty of working with this kind of business. You can make it as small or as big as you would like. Some people keep it smaller with just a few products for sale. Others decide to grow this into a large business with hundreds of products that they want to sell. And scaling it in this manner is so easy. You simply do a bit of research and decide what other products you would like to sell on your chosen sites and then you list them. That is all there is to it! It's no wonder that so many people want to figure out how to work with dropshipping; it can easily go from a side business to a full-time income with very little work.

Easy to Automate

In the beginning, you will have to put a lot of time and effort into your business. This is necessary to get any business up and running properly. You have to find good suppliers, pick out the right products to sell, get things listed and so on. This takes up some time and can be a big reason why a lot of people give up with dropshipping early on.

But if you are able to get through the beginning work with dropshipping and you are able to be successful with growing your business, you will find that you can then change-up your business and make it more automated.

This can really help to save you a lot of time and hassle. You can get your social media posts to be automated, you can handle the orders and any emails within a few hours at any time of the day that you choose, and most of the business will run itself.

Think of how it will feel to make unlimited money with a side business where most of the work is automated! This is what most people dream about when they get started with dropshipping in the first place. You have to go through and put in the hard work from the beginning, but if you can do that, you will soon be able to automate the whole business, and this can really help things to grow.

There are so many benefits that come with starting your own drosphipping business. You can reach a global market, it doesn't cost a lot to get started, you don't have to keep inventory or worry about the overhead costs, and so much more. For those who are willing to put in the hard work to make a good income, dropshipping is the way to go!

Chapter 3: The Drawbacks of Dropshipping

Dropshipping business has a lot of things that you can enjoy. It is a great way to start earning an income on the side along with your regular line of work. You can enjoy a wide range of products to sell, you can choose how much or how little you would like to sell, and you get the freedom of choosing times to work that go around your busy schedule. With that said, there are a few drawbacks that when you decide to get into the dropshipping business, which is why only a few people have seen success with this business model. Some of the main drawbacks that you may notice with dropshipping include:

Sudden Shortages in Stock

As a dropshipper, it is your responsibility to keep up with the amount of stock that is available from your supplier. You can then keep this information updated on your shop so customers know when an item is out of stock or not.

Sometimes, this is easy to do. But around the holidays, or with a really popular item, it is hard to keep up with the numbers.

If there is a sudden shortage in the stock of an item, this can pose a problem for you. Your customers may get frustrated that they can't get ahold of that item right away. And if the customer already placed an order for that item, and then you found out that item was out of stock, this can really make it difficult on you and the customer.

The best way to handle this is to have multiple suppliers for the same item, or at least two or three suppliers with similar items. This way, if your main supplier ends up running out of a particular item, and you have customers interested, you still have some options. If the items are the same, you just switch suppliers for a time and send the item out. If the items are a bit different, you can contact the customer and give them the alternative. You can also add a little extra incentive to it as well.

Customer Service is All on You

When the customer gets upset about something, they are not going to call up or email the supplier. You are the front of the business. And for all they know, you are completely in control over that product. When things go wrong, you have to handle all of the customer service yourself.

This can get tedious and hard on some occasions. You have to handle any questions that the customer has. You have to answer emails when you get comments or questions or complaints from a customer. If there need to be any returns or exchanges, you are the one who will have to handle all of this. As one person, this can seem like a lot and can really add to the workload in some situations.

Less Control Over Your Own Business

Dropshipping is a great business to get into. You can start to earn money on products that other companies make, and you don't have to keep any inventory on hand or actually make the product yourself. But, the tradeoff here is that you have very little control over your own business. The suppliers you pick will be the ones in most control over this kind of business. And if you pick the wrong supplier, it could mean the end of your business.

As a dropshipper, you are basically listing items for sale online for other companies. You list them for higher than the supplier has them, and then you take the profits. You will have a customer place the order through you, and then you take that money and place the order through the supplier. From there, the supplier takes over.

If you have picked out good suppliers to work with, this process should be easy to handle. After placing your order, they will make the product, ship it out, and your customer will be happy. But you have very little control over this. It is possible that the supplier could send the product to the wrong place, orders can get mixed up, and more. And when these happen, you have to handle the downfall, even though you didn't have control over any of it.

Potential Issues with Quality Control

Since you are not the one making the product and you never actually touch the product, there could be problems with the quality of the product. The supplier will often try to do the best they can because that is how they make money as well. But if there are quality control issues, you are the one who is going to get harmed the most. Your customers will leave bad reviews, and there isn't really much you can do since you don't make the product.

There are a few things that you can do to make sure that you provide high-quality products to your customers. First, when you are looking for a supplier, do some research on them. Look around and see what other dropshippers have thought about the products. Look and see if there are any major problems with that company that you should be worried about. If there are a lot of bad reviews, or other issues, choose to go with someone else.

Before you decide whether you are going to sell a particular product or not, consider ordering one for yourself. This way, you can get a good feel for the experience the customer will have if they order through you. You can check how the shipping is, check in with the customer service, and see how the product actually works when you have it in your hand. Do this any time you decide to work with a new supplier for your business.

Hard to Find Products That Will Make Enough Money

One challenge that a lot of dropshippers will run into is finding a product they can make a good profit margin on. There are tons of companies and suppliers who will work with this kind of business model, but you have to make sure that you pick out a product that is worth your time to sell. If you look at the price from the supplier and the product is listed as $10, but everyone online is charging $10.50, then this is probably not a good product for you to sell because you will have to sell quite a few to make anything for your time.

Many companies are like this, which is why dropshipping sometimes gets a bad name. It is important to take your time and not rush into the product that you want to work with. The bigger the margin, the easier it is for you to make a good deal of profit on it, and the more worth your time it is.

Don't waste your time making just $0.50 on each item that you sell. By the time you put in the work, do your social media, and pay the fees for the listing site, you will end up losing money. Find products that make as much as possible. For example, if you are able to find a product that costs $50 from the supplier, but other similar sellers have it listed online at $200, then this is definitely a product you should look into.

Supplier Errors

There are times when the supplier may make an error in one of the orders that you place. They may get an address mixed up and send the product to the wrong place. They may send the wrong product to one of your customers. Or they could make some other mistake that makes the customer upset.

When you are a dropshipper, it is hard to get the supplier to take on the hassle with this one. Some of the good ones will help out with this, but the customer is still going to be mad at you if something goes wrong with one of the orders. If this happens too often, you could run into the issue of too many mistakes and bad reviews, and then no customer will want to purchase from you in the future.

It is best to find a supplier you can trust. One that is known for getting orders right and for great customer satisfaction. Remember that you are the face of the business. If you sell the product, then the customer is going to blame you for things going wrong. Even though you are only listing the product and placing the order, the customer will assume you are the one in charge of everything and will take their disappointment and frustration out on you. Picking out a good supplier who takes care of their customers can make a world of difference when it comes to how successful you will be.

While there are many benefits to choosing dropshipping as your new business, there are also a few things that you need to be aware of before starting. There is some work that comes with this kind of business. And even though the income potential can be high, you do have to put in the time and effort to find a good supplier, someone who has great customer satisfaction, creates a high-quality product, and who will get the orders to the right people each time. If you are able to do that, you can easily avoid some of the negatives that come with dropshipping.

Chapter 4: How to Get Started with Your Dropshipping Business

Now that we know a bit more about dropshipping and why it is such a great business to get started with, it's time to look at the different steps that you can follow to get your business up and running. We will look at how to choose a niche, how to pick out products, and so much more to make this business successful for you.

How to Choose Your Dropshipping Niche

Before you get started, it's important to pick out the niche you would like to sell with. You want to find a niche that has higher demand but doesn't necessarily have numerous people selling to it yet. This can be the tricky part when it comes to starting your business. Dropshipping has become very popular and there many other sellers out there as well. Making sure that you can reach your customers in a new way can be a great way to actually make money.

The more specific you can make your niche, and the bigger the audience that comes with it, the better you will do. One misconception that comes with this business is that it's possible to be profitable and successful in any niche that you choose. But if the niche you want to work in has thousands of other sellers, how are you going to stand out from the crowd and make money? Some of the things that you can consider when picking out your own niche include:

1. Start with your own passion and interest: Tap into your interests and hobbies and see if you can come up with some good idea from there. There may be a nice market just waiting for you.
2. Scratch your own itch: The theory behind this one is that if you have a certain problem in your own life, then it is likely that someone else is dealing with the same issue. If you can find a product that will solve

that problem, then this could be the new niche that you work on.

3. Research more about the competition: Is the niche you are taking a look at oversaturated? Are you able to beat out the competition in some manner, or is it even worth beating them? The less competition you can find in a niche, the easier it will be to win and make money.

4. Make sure you pick out a profitable niche: The more profitable the niche is that you choose, the more money you can make from this business. You should always look into the profitability of any niche or product you want to work with. Remember, you want to come up with a profit margin that is at least 40 percent after shipping costs, taxes, and fees. If it doesn't meet up to that, then pick a different niche.

When you are picking out a niche, it is also important to take some time to really get to know the customer that you want to work with. Each niche is going to have a different type of customer and a different demographic that you will need to concentrate your energy on. The more you know about that customer, the easier it will be to market and sell to them later on.

As you are going through things and picking out your niche, think about the type of person you want to sell your product to. If you have the time, sit down and write out to your perfect customer. If you could sell the product to any person out there, what would they be like? What gender is there, what age range, what is their job, what do they like to do in their free time, where do they live, what problems do they need to be solved, do they have a family and more.

When you have this done, you will be able to plan out your social media strategy, better pick out your platform a bit better and even have a better idea of how you want to market and use the products that you plan to sell. Having this demographic information and the perfect customer all set up and ready to go can make a big difference in providing you with a path to follow for your new business plan.

Find a Supplier

We will get into this a bit more in the next chapter, but it is important to find a good supplier to work with on your business. While you are the face of your own business and have the responsibility of taking care of your customers, the supplier will be the one who actually creates and ships out the product. Finding a good supplier can either make or break your business.

If you pick out a good supplier, things are going to work out so much better for your business. You will have someone who takes care of your customers. Someone who always has a high-quality product that is readily available and shipped out right away when the customer needs it. You will have someone who is easy to work with if there are any complaints or other issues that come up. And you will always be able to rely on them.

On the other hand, if you pick out a bad supplier or one who isn't reliable, things will become a mess. You will have unhappy customers, lots of returned products, and even issues with getting good reviews. If you really want your business to thrive and do well, then you must make sure that you pick out a supplier who is ready to properly take care of your customers.

Take your time to look through all the different suppliers who are out there. You want to find someone who is going to take care of your customers, someone who has good reviews for providing excellent service, and ones who will provide high-quality products at affordable prices so that you can still make some profits for your work. This is definitely a place where you should take your time to search around to find the right company for you.

Get Your Sales Tax ID

If you are setting up this business in the United States or in Canada, then you will probably need a sales tax ID, or a retail license, resale number, vendor's license, or a tax ID. The sales tax is a tax that is levied on all the sales of physical goods sold to consumers, and depending on where you live, it will fall somewhere between six to nine percent of the price. Most states will require that you have this kind of ID but there are some exceptions such as in Oregon, New Hampshire, Montana, Delaware, and Alaska.

It is standard for a business to pass the sales tax on to the consumer by adding it into the price that they charge. Applying for this kind of ID is easy and won't cost significant amounts. You can do it online or you can visit your local county clerk's office to get it done. To do this, you need to either be a sole proprietor (which is what a lot of people will be with this since they are a home online business), a company, or a business entity.

There are some sites, such as eBay, that don't require this kind of ID. But most suppliers and wholesalers will want you to have this before they even consider doing business with you. It is best to have this number in place to make things easier when they are doing taxes at the end of the year.

Pick Out Your Products

Part of the process of picking out a supplier should include a look through the products that you want to sell. If you look at a supplier and find that they don't offer the type of products that you would like to sell, then that is not the right supplier for you. Always go in with an idea of the kind of products that you would like to sell.

When you first get started with this journey, you are going to be amazed at how many different products are for sale and what you can choose from. Try not to get overwhelmed or entranced by a product that seems cool but which has no market and won't make you any profits. Before you even go and look at any products, at least have some guidelines in place that you need to follow to ensure that you are going to find a profitable and valuable product to sell to your customers.

Make sure that you pick out at least a few products to sell. You don't want to take on too much at the beginning. Having a few products, especially ones that are related to each other, can help you to get the dropshipping business off the ground and do well.

Choose Your Selling Platform

Now that you have picked out the product that you want to use and you have set up the right supplier, it is time to find the platform you will use to start selling the product and making money. It is important to pick out the right selling platform if you want to have a business that is successful. But how do you make sure that you pick the right platform that works for you?

We will take some time to talk about each one in more detail in a bit, but there are a few options that seem to be the most popular when it comes to running a dropshipping business. Many people like to work with either Amazon, Shopify, eBay, or their own personal website. There are advantages and disadvantages to each one and the choice is often going to depend on your own goals and the types of products you want to sell.

Setting Up a Strategy to Bring Customers in

At this point, you already have a selling platform set up for the business, but you need to find a way to get people to come and look at the items that you are selling. This is why you need to come up with a strategy for gaining new customers. This is going to include amassed persuasion on your part and it is a combination of marketing and advertising. You can choose between doing either the fast path and paying for the customers, or the slower path that can be free. Often doing a combination of the two can be the right option. Let's take a look at both of these strategies to see how they can work.

Fast results with paid advertising

The first place you may consider advertising is on Facebook ads. Facebook is the biggest social media platform throughout the world, which means it's a great place to advertise your products and reach a bunch of people.

Facebook makes its money by promoting your business, so every customer that you get with this method is going to come with a cost. There are many reasons to choose to advertise with Facebook, including:

- It is really easy to get the process started.
- You get all the control over how much you decide to spend each day.
- You can be very specific on your demographics, such as picking out people of certain ages, locations, interests, and even relationship statuses.
- If it is used properly, you can also get results fast.
- It helps when you want to create more awareness for your brand.
- A good ad or a good boosted post has the potential to go viral.

Another option that you can go with is Google Ads. Google is known as one of the most popular of search engines out there. If you have your own online store, you want to make sure that it gets as high up on the list of Google search as possible. You can take your time and do this organically, or you can purchase ads for the store that appear near the top of the page for any of the keywords you are ranking for. Below are several reasons for using Google ads to help grow your business:

- You can achieve better exposure when it comes to search results.
- As mentioned, it is known as the largest platform for advertising throughout the world.
- You can also target demographics in a highly specific manner.
- You will find that the exposure you get with your ads with some of your high volume keywords can be amazing.

You can also choose to do marketing with a social media influencer. Influencer marketing has started to become a big part of gaining new customers, and it is definitely something that you should consider in your strategy for 2019. It can be really effective if you choose a niche that is really trendy. For example, if you are selling a handbag that has a new style, you could reach out to someone famous on Instagram and ask if they are willing to share a post with one of the bags while tagging your business.

There will have to be some agreement between you and the influencer. Potentially, just one post can bring in a lot of new followers and customers to your business. The amount you pay is going to depend on how famous the influencer is, how many people follow them, and other factors of your choices.

Slow results that are free

Now, as a dropshipper, it is important to keep your costs down a bit so that you can keep those margins up as high as possible. While it is fine to do the paid advertising listed above, it is also wise to save some of your budget and work on a more organic reach that doesn't cost you anything. This will take a bit more of your time but can really help with your budget overall.

The first option here is forum or blog marketing. With this one, you are going to find blogs or other types of forums that are related to the niche you are selling in. You want to then actively participate in any discussions that occur on that page. By working to position yourself as an authority in that niche and having a link to your website attached, you are going to find that, over time, you will increase the amount of traffic that heads to your site.

Content marketing is next on the list. In most cases, this is going to take in form as a blog on your store website, some trendy posts on Instagram, a YouTube channel, or something posted on Twitter. Content marketing is meant to involve some creative content that is valuable to your customers and it can really work to build up an audience that will hopefully become your customers. It is more about serving the audience rather than the brand, so make sure it isn't as explicit as advertising.

Social media is another option, but because so many other businesses are using it as well, it is harder to get an organic reach. Note, however, that while it is challenging, it is possible. You just need to consistently share and create great content on these channels. Over time, you will be able to build up a great following that can later be converted into the customers you need.

And finally, you should consider working with email marketing as well. This is still considered one of the most effective ways to acquire new customers. You must first set up a channel that will help you capture the email addresses that you want, such as a request at checkout for them to sign up. Once you have had a chance to build up your email list, you will have a great way to reach a large group of people when you need, for free.

As you can see, dropshipping is a simple idea that anyone can get started with. It isn't meant to be complicated or hard to work with. And it isn't meant to be exclusive to anyone who wants to give it a try. If you just follow the steps above, you will be able to see some great results with your own dropshipping business as well.

Picking the Right Price

Another important aspect of your dropshipping business that we need to discuss here is how to price your items the right way. Many beginners have trouble with this because they want to price it at a point where they can be attractive to the buyers and beat the competition but they also want to make sure that their price margin is high enough that the work is worth their time. Here, we will take a look at how to pick out the right pricing to make sure you get the most out of your business.

First, you do not want to price the item too high. Sure, this may make your price margin seem higher. But if your pricing is much higher than the competition, then customers will notice. They will wonder why your pricing is so high, and most of them are going to choose the cheaper option if the products are the same. The profit margins may look higher, but you aren't going to end up with any sales so you don't really want to do this at all.

Another trap that you need to avoid with this is pricing too low. Pricing a bit lower than the competition isn't bad but it still isn't the best practice to go with. The first issue with this is that you are cutting your price margin when you price it too low. The lower you price the item, the less you are able to make a profit for it. If you would like to earn a good income from this, then you need to try and make as much as possible on the items you sell.

Another issue with pricing too low is that it can make the customer wary of purchasing from you. Yes, customers like to get a good deal when it comes to purchasing any item. But when they see your price is way below the competition, they may worry that the product is something different or that it is lower quality than the others. When you price too low, it's likely that the customer will choose to go with the competition.

It is best to take a look at what the competition is pricing their items at, and then try to stay somewhere near there. This helps you earn as much as possible on the items that you want to sell but still make your items attractive to the customer so they will purchase them from you.

Chapter 5: How to Pick a Supplier and How to Pick Out a Product

Two of the most important things that you will need to do with your business is to pick out a good supplier to work with and a high-quality product to offer to your customers. These two are the basis of a good dropshipping business, and if you don't take the time to get them in place, your new business isn't going to get anywhere very fast.

There are a number of things that you will want to look into when it comes to picking out a good supplier and a good product to help you get your business up and running. Some of the things that you should consider when picking out both of these include:

How to Pick Out a Good Supplier

The entire model of this business is going to be based on the idea that the supplier will be able to do their job well and that they will work to fulfill all their orders punctually and efficiently. This is why picking out the right supplier is so important when it comes to growing your own business. If your supplier ever makes a mistake and messes up one of the orders, you, as well as your business, are the ones who are going to be responsible for this. The key here is to make sure that you find a seller that not only sells a good product but one that will also take care of your customers.

There are a few factors that you should consider when it comes to choosing a supplier for your business. The first thing to look into is finding a company that is experienced, one who has some sales representatives who know what they are doing. This can help any time you get stuck with something, when you have a question, and with other concerns. A company who knows what they are doing and has a reputation for doing it well can be a big asset to your business.

The next thing that you can look for in your supplier is to find one who can provide you with excellent products. The better the product, the higher the level of customer satisfaction. This is great news for you. It not only means some great reviews on your page and more sales, but it also means a much lower rate of returned items and unhappy customers.

If you can, it is also a good idea to find a supplier who has some technical abilities. You want to work with a supplier who has the right technological capabilities to keep up with the times. At some point, you will want to scale your business. You don't want to end up breaking off with a business partnership with the supplier simply because they wouldn't be able to keep up with the growth that you are working for.

And finally, you want to work with a supplier who is punctual and who can be efficient with their shipping process. You should pick out a supplier who is regular with shipping, someone who can ship out the products within 24 to 48 hours after placing the order. This can help ensure that you get happy customers. Since there is so much competition in the market, longer shipping times are generally bad for your customers.

If you are worried about how long the shipping time will be, consider placing a test order ahead of time. This gives you the experience of your customer through the whole process. You can see how long the shipping takes, how the product looks when it gets there, and more. This can go a long way in helping you choose which supplier you would like to work with.

How to Pick Out the Right Products to Sell

To have a successful dropshipping business, you need to make sure that you are picking out the right products to sell. There is no guaranteed way to find the perfect products for your business. However, you need to make sure that you aren't picking out items that are already being sold by a bunch of people, and also items that have a high demand so you can make some money in the process.

Each business is going to be different, so finding the right products for your needs can sometimes prove to be a big challenge. But there are a few criteria you can consider following to help you decide whether a product is going to work well for your business.

The first thing to consider is the retail price of that item. The wholesale and retail price of the product are going to be crucial. You want to hit a sweet spot in the way you price the products. Having a product at a lower price may encourage more sales, but you aren't going to make a big profit margin on those products. On the other hand, items that are priced higher may sell fewer items, but you will earn a bigger profit from each one.

As a business owner, it is important that you find a good balance that works the best for you and for the expectations of your customers. You want to make sure that you get a profit margin that is somewhere between 15 to 45 percent (or higher if you can) to ensure that the work you put into the sale is actually worth it all.

The next thing that you should consider is the size and weight of the item. The packaging and the shipping costs are going to vary based on each product, the effort it takes to ship the product, and how much packaging material will be needed. In this sense, the smaller and the lighter items are often the best to dropship because they will give you a bigger profit margin. You can find larger products that fit in with this as well, but often starting out with smaller items is the best.

Cross-selling is going to become very important to your business. Selling a set of products that are related can be a great way to provide some value to your customers, and it can encourage them to purchase more each time they place an order. If you only have one item available in each category, it is going to be hard to do any cross-selling at all. When picking out a product, consider what other products you could sell with it to serve your niche. For example, if you sell easels, you may want to also sell paint brushes, canvases, and other art supplies because it is more likely that your customers will want to purchase these kinds of items as well. When you choose to go with this option, consider the ways that you can price the products in a strategic way to make the sale worth as much value for your business as it will for the customer.

You also need to make sure that you pick out products and goods that are going to meet customer expectations. If the products or the goods you sell are renewable or disposable, there is a better chance that the customer will come back and place a repeat order, which can increase your sales. This is why so many retailers will set up a subscription option for their customers to ensure that they keep getting a repeat purchase. If you want to really impress your customers, offer a good discount to customers who are going to subscribe to the product or service you offer.

In addition to this, you need to make sure that your product is as durable as possible. You do not want to send your customers products that don't work in the manner that they should, or products that fall apart and don't work at all. This is the worst way to retain your customers and will end up with you getting bad reviews in the process. Always make sure that you are getting products that are going to impress your customers, not ones that will turn the customer away from you.

And finally, you need to take a look at the turnover rate of the products. As a retailer working through an online store, you will find that the majority of the business you get will come from the copy/content and the photography of the product that you publish on the website. These can be time-consuming and will cost you some money as well.

This means that if you decide to go with products that are going to change soon, then you will have to spend more time switching up the content to keep up. This will result in more time and money wasted. And since you have to do it all physically, it can be stressful. It is best if you find a product that has a low turnover in order to ensure that you can get the most out of the products you sell and the work that you do.

Picking out the right supplier and the right products to start your business is critical. This is going to really determine how well your business is able to do overall and how much money you are able to make in the process as well. Take your time to pick out a good supplier who will take care of you and find products that are in demand, aren't found in a saturated market, and that will earn you a good margin on your profit. If you can do this, you have most of the work accomplished for starting your dropshipping business.

Chapter 6: How to Handle Your Customers and Provide Exemplary Customer Service

The biggest thing to remember when you want to create a long-lasting and sustainable dropshipping business is to maintain a good reputation with your customers. This is all going to come down to the experience that your customer has with you and your product. Sometimes you will find that it is hard to build up that trust with your customers since the whole business is online and there is no face-to-face interaction with your customers.

But when you are starting your dropshipping business, you need to take the reigns and all of the responsibility for how well the customer service of your business is handled. Your suppliers are the ones who will take care of fulfilling all the orders. And if you picked a good supplier, you should find that part of the process good. However, the supplier is never going to have any contact with the customer. This means that you need to be the one who provides good customer service in order to keep your business growing strong.

You are the One Responsible

The first thing that you have to keep in mind with this business is that no matter how well it is all running, there will be times when things will go wrong. This can happen even for the best companies out there. Even the most trusted suppliers will run into trouble on occasion. But in the dropshipping business, when this does happen, you are the one who needs to go through and fix that situation.

In some cases, this may mean that you will lose some money to fix an order. But this loss of money is going to pay off in the long run. Fixing the mistake, even at a cost, means that you will have a customer who is more likely to come back. And they may even leave a more favorable review, rather than a bad review, to help your business grow a bit more in the future.

Understand Your Customers

If you are able to understand the wants and the needs of your customers, then this will be a big factor when it comes to how well you are able to provide customer satisfaction in your business. Your customers want to feel secure when they shop with you. Making sure that your customers have a safe and secure checkout and that they will have their personal information safe when they shop with you can be very valuable to your customers.

How do you do this? If you aren't using sites like eBay and Amazon, and you choose to sell on your own website, make sure that you build one that looks professional. Customers will run the other way if the website doesn't look professional and looks like it has been thrown together (this is a big sign of someone who is out to steal their information). In addition, on your personal website, you should consider adding in some extra security features to show customers that you value their personal information.

Know About Your Products

Customers are never happy when they purchase a product and it comes in completely different from what they expected. They are going to be mad at you and possibly even leave a bad review if they end up getting something that wasn't what they expected at all. Make sure that you provide very detailed and good product descriptions to your customers and take pictures that actually showcase the product well.

Moreover, you can add in a few other parts to help answer any questions that the customer may have. Starting an informative blog, making sure there is a good FAQ page on the website, and even sending out a newsletter on a regular basis to explain products and other information can be helpful to your customers. Remember, the less that a customer has to come to you to ask a question, the more comfortable they are going to feel when they make the purchase and the less work you have to do. If you offer the knowledge for free, they are going to appreciate that, and they will see you as more of an expert on those products and that niche.

Happiness is the Top Priority

And finally, remember that a happy customer is the best when it comes to growing your own business. Transactions that are successful and have very little friction are going to lead to happy customers. Happy customers are most likely to come back, leave positive reviews, and tell their friends about the product. All of these things will lead to your business growing and you make more money.

As you are working with your customers and creating a good experience for them, remember that a happy customer can be one of the best tools for marketing your brand out there. Treating your customers well and making them happy can help you to get your business out of there. It will also help your business grow much better than it would with any of the other tactics that we have discussed in this guidebook.

An unhappy customer can do the opposite. They will still leave reviews and share information about you with their friends and family. But often this information will be in a negative light that you do not want. Negative word of mouth spreads faster than positive word of mouth. So take the customer service of your business seriously and try to avoid any problems before they happen. And if these problems do happen, and they will at some point, do your best to handle them in a way that can satisfy your customer. Customer service is completely your responsibility when it comes to your dropshipping business. Making sure that you always take care of the customer and that you are willing to handle any of their questions, complaints, and concerns can make a big difference in how the customers feel when purchasing you, whether they will share information with others about the business, and also if they will become repeat customers.

How to Set Yourself Apart from the Competition

When it comes to dropshipping, you will see there is plenty of competition out there. Not only are there other companies selling the exact same product that you are, but there are also other individuals selling those products and other similar ones that can fit the same kind of demographic as you. It is important that you find some methods that help you to stick out from the crowd to get customers to find you and to ensure that you will get them to come back.

There are different methods that you can use to make this happen. And often, it will depend on the products that you are selling and the type of business plan you follow. One thing to note is that lowering the price too much is usually not a good method to use. Yes, it may mean that you can offer a price that is much lower than what the competitors can do, but this often backfires. Many customers will be worried about why you price so low, thinking that you are selling a substandard product. This can harm your sales. Plus, when you price things lower, you can end up with lower price margins, and it is harder to make the profits that you want.

It is better to find other methods that can help you to stand out from the competition, methods that show that you are ready to provide exceptional products and customer service to all of your customers, without having to hurt your bottom line too much.

One option that you can consider is starting a subscription service. If your product lends itself well to this, you could offer a discount to customers who agree to sign up for a few months of your service or product. This is a great way to get repeat customers and can make things easier for the customer since they can continue to get the product sent to them automatically when they need it each month.

Depending on the type of supplier you choose to use, you may want to add something special to the packaging that you send out to the customer. Adding in a personalized note to it or finding a way to showcase your business entity can go a long way for you to showcase your work and feel like there is that personal touch. If you can't do this with your supplier, another option would be to get the email address of the customer and send them a personalized message in this manner. This helps the customer to feel valued and provides you with the start of your own email list that you can use later.

As a business owner, you will soon find that positive word of mouth can go a long way in growing your business. If a customer takes the time to share your products with their friends and is willing to talk up the product, then you are more likely to make sales in the future. You can choose to use this to your advantage to make more sales.

When a customer finishes their order, ask them to share the word. You can ask them to refer a friend or place a little advertisement on Facebook or another social media site talking about their experience. Many businesses choose to offer discounts, such as 10 percent off the next purchase if their customers are willing to do this. It may cost a bit out of your pocket, but it can result in a high number of sales if you can get a few customers to agree to help you. it is well worth the investment as well.

With some types of products, you may find that it is helpful to put add-ons with it to sell more. You can offer it as a special gift that goes with the product or make some bundle deals to help make things easier for your customers when they are shopping. Customers love to be able to save money on their purchases and they love one-stop shopping. If you can provide them with a place where they can get several items that they need in one place, and you can offer your customers a discount on buying the items altogether, you can earn a big profit in the process as well.

Any time that you are able to add some freebies in with your sales, you should consider doing it. Maybe if you are selling a technology item, sending off a pamphlet with tips on how to use it, or your own personalized manual to help them use the item can make a difference. Or, if you are selling a product for making life easier in the kitchen, you can also send out a recipe book with the product to your customer.

The point here is that you want to find some ways that you can differentiate yourself from the competition. There are always going to be other people out there selling products, and sometimes they will even sell the same product that you are. You have to find a way to provide more value to the customers than that which they are getting from the competition or they have no reason to choose you over someone else.

If you are unsure of ideas on how to set yourself apart, go and look at what the competition is doing. See what the best sellers are doing in your industry and decide what you like and don't like then implement these ideas into your own strategy. You will be amazed at the different things that other competitors are doing in your industry, and taking the time to learn from them a bit can really help you to see the best results in your own dropshipping business when you first get started.

Providing good customer service can be so important when it comes to your new business. And this customer service is going to come in a bunch of different shapes and sizes. If you are able to provide an exceptional product at a good price and find other ways to beat the competition on the same or similar items, then you are well on your way to seeing success when you get started with this business model.

Chapter 7: How to Handle Security Issues With Your Business

If you choose to create your own website and sell your products through there, there's another step that you have to handle when it comes to your customers. Any customer who chooses to purchase through your website expects that website to be as safe as possible. They don't want to provide you with payment and personal information, just to find out that someone can come and steal that information right after. As a business owner, it is your responsibility to set up the site so it is secure and so your customers can shop with peace of mind.

Select a Platform that is Secure

The first thing you can do to help protect your customers is to select a platform for your site that already has some security built in. There are different platforms out there that you can choose from, but pick out one that offers PCI-compliant payment gateways and SSL security throughout the site.

Another thing that you should look for on your platform is a checkout page that is secure. You also need to make sure that there is a session timeout function so that when the user isn't active for a certain amount of time, the session will log them out to keep them safe. The more security features that you can find on your chosen platform, the better it is for your customers.

Set Higher Standards for Passwords

One of the best ways that you can make sure that your customers are shopping as safe as possible online is to insist that they use strong passwords. It is common for users to use the same kind of password on more than one account, or going through and picking something that is simple just so they won't forget it later. However, these kinds of passwords make it easy for cyber crooks to get information and it can make things even more difficult from a security standpoint.

While you can't do much about your customers using the same password that they have on another site, you can set some requirements that ensure the passwords they pick for this website are complex. For example, enforce a minimum number of lowercase and uppercase letters and add in symbols to help keep the website and the user account as safe as possible.

Protect Against Any DoS Attacks

As you will quickly see with your own e-commerce site, you will see that the DoS attacks can be a very big threat against your website. And if they are done effectively, they can keep genuine customers from getting onto your website when they need access.

DoS stands for denial of service. This kind of attack is when a hacker is going to get on a system and deliberately inundate a site, sending over more requests than that site is able to handle. The website is going to be overwhelmed and it won't be able to respond to anything at all. The hacker is then able to use some backdoor techniques in order to cause issues, steal information, and do what they want while the system is down and real customers are not able to get onto the site.

To help avoid his issue, you can use a mitigation service. This service is able to filter out the traffic that comes into your website and it will check to see that the requests that are coming in actually are done by real people rather than from bots. This is a simple way to help prevent against a large-scale attack that could really put your business and the personal information of your customers at risk when they visit your site.

Use an SSL Protection Layer

And finally, adding in a layer of protection with SSL can be a great way to keep your website site. Since you are an e-commerce business, you will have to collect sensitive customer information to complete the transactions and receive payment. This means that you will have access to the customer name, their address, and their credit card or other payment information. This is all just part of the e-commerce business.

As a business owner in this industry, it is important for you to protect all of this information as much as you can. This is where the SSL protection is going to come into play. The SSL, or Secure Socket Layer, is able to encrypt any information that is sensitive as it travels from the customer (point A) to you (point B). This encryption is going to make it harder for any outsider to come in and intercept the information.

SSL is actually the standard when it comes to using websites online, especially when sensitive information is shared between two parties, so you need to make sure that you have it in place on your website. In fact, most customers are going to look for the padlock sign on their browser before they make a purchase to make sure that their information won't be stolen. If you don't have this in place, you will lose out on a lot of customers.

In addition to providing your customers with some extra peace of mind when it comes to shopping online with you, the SSL protection may even be able to give your site a boost in SEO. This helps you to get seen by more customers and makes it easier for your business to grow.

Protecting the information of your customers can be very important when you sell any item online and when you are growing your business. You want to make sure that your customers will feel safe and secure when they come to your website, and that they will come back again and again. Make sure to put as much security on your business website as possible to ensure that customers can shop and make payments without worry.

Chapter 8: How to Scale Your Business

When you first get started with your dropshipping business, you will probably work with just a couple of products. This helps you to learn the ropes, try a few things out, and get used to everything. But over time, you will want to scale your dropshipping business and make it grow. After you have gained some experience, you will be able to add in more products, and really see the business, and your income, grow.

The nice thing about dropshipping is that you can scale it to be however big you would like and you can choose how quickly you would like to scale the business as well. This chapter is going to show you a few of the strategies that you can use in order to scale your business and make as much money as you would like with this revenue stream.

Add More Products to Your Inventory

The best way to scale your business is to just add more products to your list. You can go through the supplier you like to use and pick out a few different items that you want to add to your site. You can choose to go with something that is completely new or find other items that can complement the items that you are already selling.

As a business owner, it is best to just add in a few products at a time. You don't want to overwhelm yourself with some of the work that can come, and each product can add in a lot more work for you. If you have ten products, it's not a good idea to instantly jump to selling forty products overnight. Adding in five or six new products, seeing how that goes, and then adding in more can be a great way to ensure you are prepared for the extra work.

The nice thing about your dropshipping business is that you are able to scale this business as large as you would like. If you only start out with a few products but want to grow it to have 100 products over time, this is possible with dropshipping. Just make sure to only take on as much as you can handle and still provide good customer service at the same time.

Consider Seasonal Items

If you are working on a few products that seem to be doing well and you now want to see about scaling the business to make it bigger, seasonal items can be a great option. These are items that sell well during a certain time of the year but won't be available all the time. Things like beach items, Christmas items, or Halloween items can do well with this. When you want to scale your business, these products can be nice to work with. They allow you to sell items that are really popular and unique and there can be a good margin on them if you pick the right ones. You can get some experience with selling more items, but then you still have times when you get a break during the process as well.

If you are going with seasonal items, make sure that you start selling them early. If you start selling them just a week before the holiday or before that season, you are too late to the party and you have missed out. Starting earlier than other sellers is a great way to get more customers and get your name at the top of search engines for these items. Also, try to find items that are unique rather than selling the same items that other competitors to put yourself ahead of the competition.

Hire Others to Help You Manage the Business

Over time, as you sell more products and gain more inventory, you may find that you are making enough in profits that you are able to hire on some help to do some of the work. This is when your business has really started to do well. In the beginning, you will be in charge of everything. You have to pick which suppliers and which products you want to sell. You have to take the time to list the products with good product descriptions in place. You have to process the orders and get them shipped off to the right people. And you have to handle any issues or questions the customers may have.

As you start to grow your inventory more, you will find that doing this and keeping up with other things in your life can be really hard to handle. You need to keep doing the same process no matter how many products you add to your inventory. And you may find that it is easier to hire a team to help you do the work and manage things for you.

Before you jump in and do this, make sure that you make a high enough margin that it makes sense to hire others to help you. If hiring someone else is going to eat up all of your profits, then it doesn't make sense to hire someone to help. But once you have expanded out your products quite a bit and you have a steady customer base, then it may make sense to hire someone to help you out on occasion to free up some of your time.

Many people want to make a full-time income out of dropshipping, but very few people want to actually spend all day working on this business. Once your business starts getting to the point where you have trouble keeping up with it by working a few hours a night, then you are well on your way to scaling the business. Hiring some help can make sense to free up your time. This helps to ensure that you still get a nice income while only working part-time in the process.

As your business keeps on growing, you may find that you need to hire more and more to help the business grow. Your dropshipping business can grow as fast and as big as you would like. You just need to properly manage the business, handle customer issues properly, and work to grow the business in the right manner. As the business grows, hiring people to help manage your products can make a big difference while still helping you to make a full income in the process.

Chapter 9: How to Dropship with Shopify

There are a lot of different platforms that you can choose to use when it comes to starting your dropshipping business. One of the popular options that you can choose to use for this kind of business is Shopify. Shopify is a commerce platform that is going to help you start, grow, and even manage your business. There is so much that you can love about Shopify and how it can help your business to grow.

With Shopify, you get the benefits of creating and then customizing your own online store. Once you have that set up, you are able to sell in a bunch of different places at once. You can choose to work with selling online, mobile selling, social media, online marketplaces, brick and mortar companies, and even with some pop-up shops.

Shopify is completely cloud-based and hosted. What this means is that you are able to create your own e-commerce site and then not have to worry about upgrading at any time or maintaining the web servers and software along the way.

This is great for many business owners who are not able to keep up with web hosting and all the maintenance that goes with running their own site. Shopify also helps you have all the flexibility that you need in order to run your business from anywhere as long as you have a connection to the internet.

Dropshipping on Shopify can be a great choice. It helps you to increase the market that you are able to work with. You simply need to pick out a Shopify plan and have some products that you want to sell. Shopify doesn't care if you are using products that you make or if you choose to dropship just as long as you are able to provide details on your products when you get started.

When you work with Shopify, you are basically setting up your own online store using web hosting and other services that this company is able to offer you. You can easily try out the company for a few weeks for free, even without a credit card. So even if you decide not to use this option, it is still worth your time to check it out. If you do decide to try out this option more permanently, there are a lot of paid options that help you to start your online store to sell unlimited products through many different sales channels based on your personal budget.

In addition to having a lot of different sales channels that your products will be available through, which can increase your reach, you will also get the benefit of 24/7 support and the security that your customers are looking for when it comes to keeping their personal and payment information safe.

Getting started with Shopify is pretty easy and many dropshippers find that this is one of the easiest and cost-effective methods to get their business started, especially if they want to go through the process of creating an online store. The first step after picking out your supplier and your products is to pick out which product you want to use through Shopify. There are a few options, and it depends on how much you want to spend a month and how much support and services you want. All of them offer an online store, unlimited products, 24/7 support, multiple sales channels, and free SSL certificate. Some of the more expensive plans allow you to pay less on credit card rates and can cost you less in commissions for each of the transactions that you do.

Once you have the right plan for your use of Shopify, it is time to pick out your template. Shopify can provide you with a lot of different templates that you can use. As a beginner, you may want to go with one of these templates because it makes things easier. You can also choose to pick out some of your own templates or create your own if you don't find one that works the best for your needs. Take your time to look through all the different options that are available. This will ensure that you find one that will be easy for your customers to use and one that works with the products that you sell.

Make sure to take the time to pick out a good template and go through and start to list out all of your products. All of the plans that are available through Shopify allow you to put unlimited amounts of products on the site, so go ahead and list as many products as you would like. Because of this, you will also be able to go through and use Shopify in order to scale your business because it is easy to add in more products later on.

If you already have your own domain name, you can use that along with Shopify. You will be able to connect your existing domain name when you get onto your account from the store admin. Or, if you don't have a domain name yet, Shopify makes it easy to get this all set up and working for your needs.

As you are adding in the products to your account, make sure to bring in excellent pictures. This is the first thing that a lot of people are going to see and these will help you draw in more customers as well. Each product posting needs to have a good description added to it, perhaps with a few keywords, to ensure that you are actually selling the product and that your customer will be able to find the product when they search for products like yours.

When you are creating your Shopify page, remember that it is going to be shared across a lot of different platforms. This is part of the benefit of working with this website, but it also means that you need to be careful about the work that you do. You need the products to sell across all of these platforms, so pick out high-quality pictures, good descriptions, and has all the information that the customer may need before making a purchase.

Shopify will work with a third party payment processor to help you handle the payments for all of your products. This ensures that both you and the customer are going to be protected during the process and can work the best since you are able to reach customers all over the world. Once you receive an order for one of your products through Shopify, you will receive a notification about it. The way you get the notification is going to depend on your settings. You can get an RSS notification, text message, or email after each order. When you are looking for a method of selling your products in a multitude of ways and you want to reach your customers wherever they may be, then Shopify is the best choice to go with. There are a lot of options that come with it. It can help you to reach your customers through social media, online, in person, and more, and the plans are very affordable.

Chapter 10: How to Dropship On Amazon and eBay

Two of the biggest platforms that dropshippers will use to help sell their products are Amazon and eBay. Both of these platforms are household names, which makes them the perfect options for getting your products out there. There are times when competition may be an issue. But if you plan things right and pick out unique and high-quality products, it is still possible to make a lot of money with these platforms. This chapter will take a look at some of the steps that you can take in order to get your own dropshipping business up and running on eBay and Amazon.

Dropshipping on Amazon

Amazon is one of the biggest platforms that is used for dropshippers. It is usually pretty easy to sell items on the site, it reaches millions of people throughout the world, and the fees usually aren't too bad for most sellers to handle.

Working with Amazon is pretty simple to use and almost anyone is able to work with this method as well.

To get started with dropshipping on Amazon, you first need to set up a seller account. You can choose to just start selling off your regular account or you can set up a separate one to help you keep things separated as well. At this point, you should already have your products picked out, so now it is time to list them. Just go to your seller account and start listing.

Just like with any platform you choose to use, it is often best to take your time when listing. You want to have high-quality pictures, ones that will show the customer the product well. Remember that the customer can't go to a physical store and actually touch and turn the product around. If you already own the product, consider taking your own pictures rather than using stock images. If you can find some unique way to showcase the product, something different than what the competitor is doing, then you should consider doing that as well to entice more customers.

Writing a good description is important as well. You want to make sure that the description is actually able to sell the product, that it is there to entice the customer to actually purchase that product. Using persuasive language, adding in some keywords, and showing the customer how this product can help solve a problem for them can all be great ways to write convincing copy to get more sales from the posting.

Amazon will usually charge based on the sale price of the item. You will have to give them about ten percent for most products that you sell. It is important to count this into your profit margin when you are picking out products. Only earning one percent on an item after Amazon takes their cut isn't really going to make this process worth your time. Even though the fees may seem a bit higher with Amazon compared to some of the other options, there are a lot of benefits to working with this site. The biggest advantage is that you are putting your products with a brand that is really recognizable. Amazon is now a household name throughout the world, and you won't have to spend time telling your customers how its marketplace works. And since it is such a big company, you won't have to worry so much about some of the little things like SEO, marketing, and advertising just to get people to the website.

When you sell your products in this manner, you can sell your products without having to pay for them ahead of time or having them sit around and not getting sold. You will only have to pay for an item once it is sold. Amazon is really good at making this process as easy and painless as possible. While there are a few fees, selling with dropshipping and through Amazon is a much cheaper option than holding inventory and spending for that.

In addition, Amazon makes it easier for you to expand with your virtual inventory. You can easily add in as many products as you would like to your store. Amazon doesn't have a limit to how much you can sell with them, which makes it easier to scale your business without having to worry about moving platforms or changing other things.

There are a few requirements that you must meet in order to sell on Amazon though. These include:

- You need to be the seller of record for all of the products.
- You need to identify yourself as the seller of the products on any information that is provided or included with the product.
- You need to be responsible for accepting and processions customer returns on all of the products for your customers.
- And you have to know all of the selling policies through Amazon and agree to comply with these terms.

The good news is that most of these are already going to be done for you when you sign up with your suppliers. As long as you stick with the rules and don't try to cheat the system, you will be able to get your dropshipping business up and running with Amazon.

Dropshipping on eBay

The next place we are going to look for starting a dropshipping business is through eBay. There are a lot of buyers who like to head over to eBay because it is a simple platform to work with and they can get some good deals. If you feel that your buyers are going to be in this area, or you feel like your product would be best suited for working on eBay, then this is definitely a place for you to start with your business.

If you would like to start your dropshipping business on eBay, the first thing that you need to do is create a seller account on eBay. When you get started on this site, you will have to create a seller account. When you post an item, you will have to pay a small listing fee. Make sure to count this listing fee in with your investment to the business so it doesn't surprise you later on.

For those who get to this part and are still trying to figure out what they would like to sell, there are a few tools that you can use through eBay. You want to make sure that there is a high enough demand for the product but not too much supply before you decide to sell one product over another. Some of the steps that you can use in order to find out how good a product will sell includes

- Go to eBay
- Click Advanced Search
- Enter the product that you are considering
- Sort by Price highest first
- Select on completed listings only
- Click search
- From here you can take a look at the best selling products in the niche or for the product you are interested in.

Once you have chosen some of the products that you would like to sell, it is time to list them on eBay so you can start to make some money. Make sure to upload some images and good descriptions. Some beginners like to just copy and paste the description that comes from the supplier's website. This makes things easier but you need to take a look at the description first. Sometimes these are short and sometimes grammar and spelling are off. You want to really sell the product so you may want to rewrite the description using descriptive language and some top keywords for your niche.

At this time, you will also need to come up with the price you want to charge for the item. The price needs to find the right balance between being low enough that it can compete against some other items on the market but high enough that you are able to make a good profit margin, even after you pay for the listing fees for posting on eBay.

After you have paid the listing fee for that product, eBay will post the product online. You now can work on other forms of advertising in order to get more people to find your products and make the purchase as well. Once a customer finds your product and makes a purchase, you can take the payment and put that towards placing the order with your supplier. You simply give the supplier the customer's shipping address and they will take care of the rest of the work for you.

Since the eBay listing fee can cut into your profit margins a bit more, you may want to pick out a little higher margin when you choose a product you want to go with. This can help to cover the costs that you incur when you work with this site. You also can list more than one of the product to make the listing fees work more in your favor.

Both Amazon and eBay are great options when it comes to starting your dropshipping business. They can both help you reach a ton of customers and can do a lot of the advertising and work for you in the process. There are some more fees in the beginning compared to starting your own website and selling. But since these sites are well-known and do a lot of the work in the process, many dropshippers choose to at least get started with this method over some of the others.

Chapter 11: Creating a Personal Website for Your Dropshipping Business

Another method that you can use to help get your business off the ground is to create your own personal website. This method may cost a bit more in the beginning compared to the others. You have to pay for a domain name, get the website set up, and work on SEO. But once the website is up and running, it is a great way to build up a brand, and you can keep 100% of the money that you earn on your products.

Some beginners feel a bit worried about starting their own website. They feel that they would not be able to create a good website or that it is too much work. But if you are willing to put in just a bit more time and effort in the beginning, you will find that a personal website can work better than some of the other methods we have discussed so far in this guidebook.

In this chapter, we are going to take a look at how you can create one of your own personal website for this kind of business. We will use WordPress which will help keep things easy, but you can choose whichever hosting site that you are the most comfortable with. Some of the steps that you can follow in order to create your personal website to get your dropshipping business off the ground include:

Get Your Domain Name and Web Hosting

The first thing that you need to work on is getting your own domain name for the website. The domain name is going to be the unique address for your website. It is the name that a customer will type into the search engine in order to find you. Something like www.mystore.com is your domain name.

On the other hand, you also need to work with web hosting. This is a remote server that is going to store all of the data for your website and then makes that information accessible to anyone who decides to visit your site. You can think of the web hosting like a house that stores everything and the domain name is the address to that house.

There are numerous different domain names and hosting providers to help you out with this. But if you can, it is best to pick out the right one even if it costs a bit more. A good hosting provider and domain name can do a ton when it comes to how successful your website will be.

When picking out a domain name, you may need to experiment around a bit. You may already have a good name in place for your business and that can help. If not, now may be the time to think about this a little bit. In addition, you may find that some of your first choices for domain names aren't readily available because someone else has chosen them. Being flexible and trying out a few different options will ensure that you are able to find the domain name that you want to work with.

Install WordPress

Once you have picked out your domain name and your web hosting, it is time to install WordPress. There are two different forms of WordPress that you can work with. These include WordPress.com and WordPress.org. Both of these can be great options and it often depends on the amount of freedom and work you want to have. It is best to work with WordPress.org because this allows you to use your own domain name which looks more professional and ranks higher in SEO compared to the other option. On the other hand, Wordpress.com can make things easier because a lot of things are automatic.

First, let's look at WordPress.com. This option is going to offer both the regular option and the Business Plan. If you are going with this choice, then make sure that you choose the Business Plan to help grow your dropshipping business. With WordPress.com Business plan, you will have a custom domain, premium hosting, the security that your customers need, and plenty of backups to make sure your information stays up to date.

With WordPress.com, you also get a chance to pick from hundreds of customized themes or you can install your own custom theme in some cases. It is also possible for you to share the page when needed to some of the more popular social media accounts you will want to work with which can make your social media strategy a little bit easier to work with. And as a business owner, you will find that there are a lot of graphing and statistical tools that you can choose to go with to make your website strong.

If you go with this option, the pricing can be a bit higher than some of your other choices. You will also need to register for an account through WordPress.com and have to abide by the Terms of Service that are there. But if you are fine registering for this and a few of the other kinks that come with this choice, you will have a great website that is backed by a powerful name in the industry. Most of the work will be done for you, too.

If you would like to have a bit more freedom with the website and get to control everything about it, then WordPress.org is going to be the choice that you want to work with. You will get plenty of security and you can either install your own custom themes or build your own with the help of CSS and PHP. You can also get the benefit of installing plugins into the plan, such as Jetpack, to help you get more functionality for sharing the site.

Probably the biggest benefit of this one is that you are able to really work with plugins. WordPress.com Business will allow you to have a few plugins, but you can pick almost any kind that you want with the WordPress.org option. Plus, you don't have to worry about registering with WordPress.org in order to use these websites.

Of course, these are just two of the options that you can choose from when creating your own dropshipping website. You can also choose to work with other platforms if you are interested in working with different features or if you think the way the platform is laid out will work better for the products that you are trying to sell. No matter which option you choose to go with, make sure that you have full control over your hosting and your domain name. That way, if you ever run into trouble with the platform, or you choose to switch, you can still maintain control over it all.

Set Up the Website and Pick the Right Plugins

Now that you have chosen the domain name, the hosting, and the platform that you would like to use for your website, it is time to get the website set up. Just like with the other options for your website, make sure that you take the time to list all of your products and write great descriptions to go with them. Since this is a standalone website, you will need to really work on the keywords that go with the different items to ensure that you can work on SEO and draw more customers to your page.

With the other options that we chose, you had a good name behind you, one that was well known and could bring in the customers for you. That company already did the SEO and a lot of the customer reputation work so you just had to deal with making your product stand out from the crowd. But when you work with your own website, you need to find a way to make the website stand out so people are able to find you and purchase the product. High-quality pictures, good descriptions, and even a blog tied to the website can all help you to rank higher with SEO.

Since this is a personal website, your template may not just include the items that you are selling. Many personal websites will have a contact page, an introduction page that talks about the company or the products a bit, and even an About Me page. If you have a blog or plan to create one, then make sure that it is linked to the website as well.

While creating your own website, you will find that plugins can be your best friend. You will need a few of them to make your website work better. You can consider a plugin to help with recommendations for the customer, ones that help hold on to the cart and sends reminders to your customers if they leave something behind, plugins for listing similar products the customer might like, and then plugins to help with processing payment so you can place the order and get the product sent out to your customer.

As you can see, there are quite a few more steps that come with creating your own website, and this can often turn beginners off form doing this method. But while it does cost a bit more and usually takes a bit more work when you get started, it is going to pay off on the long run. Once you get the website up and running and you get a good number of customers to visit your site, you can easily scale it and make more money without having to pay more fees or other investment costs to earn the money.

Chapter 12: Do I Need to Use Social Media for My Business?

As a dropshipper in the modern world, it is important that you figure out how to work with social media to grow your reach. If you forget to start up a social media presence, then you may as well just give up on the business right away. There are a lot of people who want to get into dropshipping and they are competing against thousands of other businesses out there in order to get ahead. Social media is a great way to get the word out there to help you reach as many people as possible and to help increase your overall business.

Social media has grown in leaps and bounds in recent years, and it seems like everyone is now online for at least a little bit of their day. This provides a lot of potential for a business to share their products and make some money in the process. The biggest issue you will have to consider when getting started is which site you want to get started with.

Since there are so many social media sites that you can work with, you may feel overwhelmed at first. The good news is that you only need to pick two or three to work with, and then ignore the rest. If you try to manage ten or more social media sites in order to promote your products, you are going to run into some trouble. Doing this may sound like a good way to increase your reach, but in reality, you are spreading yourself too thin and you aren't concentrating on where your customers actually are.

So, the first goal that we want to work on here is figuring out which social media sites are the best for reaching our customers. Spend some time learning more about your customer, thinking about the way that they like to shop and where they like to spend their time. Which social media sites do you think they would spend their time on? Pick two or three sites where you are likely to find these individuals, and then work on promoting good and valuable information on each one.

One note to consider is to try out some sites that aren't Facebook. Yes, we do spend some time talking about

Facebook in this guidebook, and there are many benefits to using this site. But you shouldn't just automatically jump to this choice just because it is the largest and most well-known option. If your research shows that a few other social media sites are better for reaching your customers, then those are the ones that you should go with.

When working on your social media accounts, make sure that you concentrate on providing high-quality information and posts that provide value to your customers. There are plenty of other marketers you have to fight against on social media and your posts are going to get lost in the clutter and not get seen by anyone if you just post a bunch of junk. Find things that provide value, that are funny, and that can really get the attention of others in order to see more engagement from your posts.

Some of the other tips that you can follow in order to get the most out of your own social media strategy for your dropshipping business include:

1. Once you have been able to decide which of the social media sites you would like to use for marketing, it is time to work on ways to make your presence there effective. It doesn't do you much good to get on a site and then never have anyone see you.
    a. For example, if you decide to use Facebook, you can start by setting up a good Fan Page for this business. You can then work on making this as good as it can be, using some of the free apps available to make the page amazing.
2. When you are on the social media site, make sure that you are always consistent. You should post fresh, valuable, and relevant content to the site on a regular basis. You should try to post at least once each day. It isn't going to work for you to build up a Facebook page or an identity on Twitter, and then abandon it forever.

3. Never use these pages for the personal stuff. You want to be friendly and give off more about your brand but never share your personal details such as that bad breakup on your business social media pages. This is unprofessional and it is going to drive a lot of people away from your business.

4. If you decide to work with Facebook for your marketing, make sure that you use the Facebook Insights that are provided. These are going to be analytical tools for your Fan Page, and they are free. You can take the time to look through them and find a lot of information about user growth, demographics, and any other information that you need to help grow your business even more.

5. If you decide to work with Twitter for marketing, be sure that you go on and update your content often. You can also follow people who would be the most interested in the products you are selling. Remember that quality is always more important

compared to quantity when it comes to social media. Twittercounter can be a good free tool to work with because it will show you information about the growth, or lack of growth, that is occurring on your page.

6. Never purchase followers or fans for your social media sites. This is a big mistake that new marketers will try to do in order to help them grow their reach. But most social media sites are fighting against them and are starting to penalize marketers start to go with these paid followers and likes. If you go through and try to inflate the numbers using this method, you are going to be found, and it will end up penalizing your whole business.

Even as a dropshipping business, you will find that social media can be a very important part of growing that business. You have to find ways that are going to help you reach your customers and really get them to come into your business and purchase from you rather than from someone else. Follow these simple tips in order to really reach your audience when it comes time to sell the products that you have available.

Chapter 13: What About Using Affiliate Marketing?

As we have discussed a bit in this guidebook, there are many different ways to market and promote your dropshipping business. And as a new business owner, you need to be able to figure out which method works the best for your products and for your business. No one has an unlimited budget so you won't be able to try and get all of the different marketing avenues to help grow their business. You have to pick out the ones that are the best for you.

One method that you can choose to use that can help keep your budget on track and which ensures that you only have to pay out when a purchase has been made is affiliate marketing. Here, you let other influencers in the market take on the work of talking about and promoting your product. Then, when that influencer is successful at getting some sales for you, you can pay them an agreed upon amount.

This works out nicely for you. If an affiliate takes your link and doesn't make any sales at all, then you don't have to pay them. But if they do get a bunch of sales through their work, you earn a good profit, and they can earn an income as well. It is a win-win for both sides that ensures someone is working hard for you in the process as well.

Affiliate marketing is a pretty easy concept to get started with. The idea is that you will get other people to do the work of advertising your products for you. These individuals often own successful social media sites or blogs and they are looking for ways to monetize that. They already have done the work of building up a good presence online and they want to be able to benefit from that as well. They want a way to make money from their work and you want a way to sell more of your products. Both of you can work together to make this happen.

To get started, you will find influencers who are interested in promoting your products. There are different places you can list yourself under and then interested influencers can choose whether or not to promote your link. When you post in these sites, it is important to be as detailed as you can. Most affiliates are going to be a bit picky about the products that they are willing to sell. This is because they actually want to provide a product that their customers are going to want to use and want to buy. They don't make any money if they don't get their readers or followers to make a purchase. So the affiliate wants to make sure they are picking out the right product in the process.

During this step, take some time to really explain more about your product and what your company is about. The more details you can go into here, the easier it will be for the affiliate to decide if it is right for them and the more information they have at their disposal when they are telling their readers or followers about you. Try to think of any questions that the affiliate may have about the product or services, and include that in your description as well.

Next, you have to come up with an incentive that is worth it for your affiliate. Offering $0.05 per purchase is probably not going to get you any affiliates at all. Remember that these potential marketers have spent a lot of time on their blogs or on their pages, perhaps years or more. They want to actually make some good money in the process and they still have to go through and write posts that will showcase your product to their customers. If you place the amount too low, you aren't going to get anyone in the door to look at your products.

If you are unsure about how much you should offer as an incentive, you can do some research. Consider looking around at the competition and see how much they are offering for

their affiliate links. You want to at least be competitive in this regard in order to get good affiliates to market your products. Remember, this is beneficial to you as well because you only have to pay out if you get sales from that affiliate. You don't want to short them during this time, or you won't make any sales.

Also, when trying to figure out how much you should offer, count this into your price margin. You are going to have to take that money out of the profits that you earn. So add that into the cost for the product and the shipping for the product, and then see what your price margin is in the end. If it is still in a comfortable range after doing this, then go ahead and use the affiliate marketing program to help you earn more.

Once you have determined what product to sell, gotten a good description up about it and your company, and decided how much you would like to offer as an incentive, you have to work on the links. Many affiliate marketing sites will help you with this. But the point is that each affiliate needs to be given their own unique link back to your product.

This is a very important step. You want to make sure that you can keep track of the individual sales that they bring in. Without these individual links, you have no idea who is bringing in which customers and how much to pay each person. And for a good affiliate marketing program, you want to have at least a few marketers talking up your product. Giving each marketer their own unique link back to the product ensures that you know where the customers are coming from and that you pay each individual the amount they deserve

When an affiliate signs up and agrees to market your product, you can simply give them the unique link and they will do the rest. They may talk about the product on their blog or on their social media page, and then they will provide a link to their readers or their followers. If one of the readers or followers is interested in the product, they can click on the link and choose to purchase. At the end of an agreed upon time, such as a week, a few weeks, or a month, you will pay the affiliate marketer based on how many of their readers or followers actually made a purchase on your site. If no one purchased through the link, then you will not have to pay anything.

Affiliate marketing can be a great way to promote your business. It is beneficial for both you and for the other person. The affiliate gets the benefit of earning an income on all the hard work they have put in on their site, and you get the benefit of only paying when the advertising leads to a sale while also reaching a much bigger group of people than you can do on your own. Set up a good affiliate program with your customers and you will see your business grow in no time at all.

Chapter 14: How Amazon FBA Can Help You Grow Your Business

Another way that you can grow your business is to use Amazon FBA. This is basically Fulfillment by Amazon, where the client companies are going to store their products through the fulfillment centers of Amazon. Amazon will then pick, pack, ship, and provide the customer service for these kinds of products. The success stories of doing this are circulating like crazy, and it is one of the reasons why this method is growing so much in popularity. However, there still aren't a lot of facts about how you can get started with this kind of business, or even how to grow and scale this kind of business.

The good news is that it isn't really that hard to get this kind of business running well. The real challenge with this method is to rise above the competition and learn how to expand out this kind of business. But if you do it the right way, you may be able to really grow out your dropshipping business while also making sure that Amazon is the one taking care of everything that your supplier usually handles.

Amazon is a name that most people know and trust. Working directly with them can be great news for your business. It can help you make your customers happy because they know the product is coming from Amazon's warehouse. And you get the peace of mind knowing that Amazon is taking care of all the work, even the customer service. As a beginner or even someone who has been in the market a little bit longer, you will find that dropshipping with Amazon FBA is the best option for you.

Amazon FBA

FBA is a fantastic way for you to make some more money on the affiliate sales that you may already be doing on Amazon, assuming that you are already selling a decent amount of the same products each month. FBA is when you will ship the products to an Amazon warehouse. You can then list the products on Amazon itself, and as the products are sold, Amazon will handle packaging and the shipping to the customers. If there are any returns, Amazon can handle these as well.

Once you have been able to ship the products over to Amazon, and you have taken the time to list them on the Amazon site, there isn't much to do. You have to make sure that traffic is being driven to your site, but Amazon will take care of the fulfillment for you.

This method works best if you have been dropshipping for some time. Many people who work with Amazon expect two-day shipping or at least shipping that is fast. You do not want to wait for an order, place it, have it shipped to Amazon, and then have Amazon ship it for you. Your customer will not be happy with that long of a wait time.

But, if you have been building up your business for some time and you know the approximate number of sales that you can make from one month to another, then this method can work. You can order many products at the beginning of the month, ship it over to an Amazon warehouse, and then Amazon will take care of the rest. And since Amazon covers the shipping in most instances, you will only have to deal with that cost once.

There are a lot of benefits that come with using FBA. In addition to enjoying the name familiarity that comes with using Amazon, some of the other benefits that come with this method include:

- FBA is reliable and fast: Amazon is able to process as well as ship order at really fast speeds.
- You do not have to take on any of the responsibility of warehousing, shipping, or even dealing with your customers.
- Amazon is good at converting, or turning traffic over to sales because it has a platform that others already trust and know.

While there are a lot of good things to enjoy when you work with Amazon FBA, there are also a few negatives that you should be aware of. Some of the negatives of working with this program along with your dropshipping business will include the following:

- If you use FBA, you will have to pay for the storage of your products. If you don't end up selling the products, this can end up being expensive.
- If you don't sell the items within a six month period, then Amazon will start to charge you more per month to store the items. This is why it is a good idea to wait until you know how much you are going to be able to sell before you get started.
- The backend of using Amazon is going to provide you with limited amounts of data on where the sales and the traffic are coming from. You will run into a lot of competition who are also using this program as well.

The biggest advantage of working with FBA for your dropshipping business is that Amazon is a large platform, one that a lot of people trust. And using Amazon can make the logistics and packaging of the products a bit easier.

Amazon will handle all of the logistics, instead of you, and they are able to handle the products in a quick and efficient manner for your customers. This makes it worth it for a lot of beginners in this business.

The biggest disadvantage of using FBA with this kind of business is that you are going to have to pay to use it. Amazon is going to take a bit of the sales that you earn and they are going to charge for warehousing the products, for packaging, and for the delivery of the product. This can quickly add up and will make it hard to earn a good amount of profit in the process.

If you are able to find a product, or products, that have a good profit margin for you to work with, and you would like to make Amazon do the work after the business has grown quite a bit and you want to take a break from the work, then working with FBA is a great option. There are a few things that you should consider and remember when you are ready to get started with adding FBA to your dropshipping business including:

- If you want to compete on Amazon, you have to remember the pricing. Unless the product is truly special, which isn't likely, the price is one of the only things that will help you set apart from the other retailers out there selling the same product.
- Avoid a price war: It is hard to compete on the search results through Amazon. It is best to find ways to drive traffic over to your own personal landing pages with Facebook Ads and SEO.
- Targeted traffic is going to convert the best: If you are able to drive traffic to the product listing, it is going to work well for you. This is true even if you don't have the best product or the cheapest product. Buyers who are searching for that product keyword are going to be ready to buy at that time. if you can capture them and make sure they get to the landing page for your products, you have a better chance of seeing conversions.

- If your margins are low, you have to sell a lot: It is best to find products that can make more money with each sale. This may seem harder to do, but the amount of time and effort that you put into the smaller and less expensive items are just not going to be worth your time. if you can, find items that will make it easy to earn $100 or more on each sale.

- Remember that some products are only seasonal. If you had a good month in July, remember that this doesn't automatically mean you are going to be successful in August. You have to learn what the different seasonal items are and then plan accordingly so you know when it will be a good month and when it will be a bad month.

- Don't run out of inventory. When you run out of inventory, it can take some time to restock depending on the supplier you used and other options. Each day you are not providing the item to customers, you are missing out on making money. But then you need to find a good balance with this because you don't want to keep around too much of the product or it will cut into your margins thanks to the cost of warehousing all the products.

- FBA can be hard. You have to put in the work to make this one happen. And for some people, even the benefits are not enough to convince them to go with it. If you do decide to go with Amazon FBA, realize that you have to go through and drive traffic to your particular page. There are a lot of other dropshippers and suppliers who are using this tool as well, and it is up to you to make sure that customers will find and use you, rather than relying on the competition.

Amazon FBA can be a great resource that will help you to grow your business. It can also take out some of the work that you end up doing when dealing with the customers and providing good service. But it is definitely something that needs to wait until you can build up the business and get enough orders to make it worth it since Amazon will charge a bit for using their services. You have to take a look at Amazon FBA and decide if it is the right choice for the business that you are running or if you need to try something else.

Chapter 15: Tips to Make Your Dropshipping Business As Successful As Possible

Now that we have taken some time to look into dropshipping and how to start your own business, it is time to take a look at a few tips that you can follow in order to get the most out of this business model. Dropshipping is a simple idea, but it does take some work to get things up and running. Some of the tips that you can follow in order to make your business as successful as possible include the following:

Focus on the Marketing

When you get started with your own dropshipping company, you have to take some time to focus on marketing. Even if you plan to list on Amazon or eBay, you still have to spend some time marketing your products in order to stand out from the crowd. There are many other sellers and dropshippers out there who are trying to compete for the same market as you. if you don't take the time to market your products and your page, you will end up getting lost in the crowd and won't make any sales.

We talked about a lot of different ways that you can market your products, and as a business owner, it is important that you learn about how each one can help you grow and scale your own business now. You may find that SEO is the best choice for you, especially if you do your own personal website to sell the products. You may find that spending some time on social media is a better option. Many new companies like to work with email marketing to see their results show with previous customers.

All of the methods can work well. But if you are able to think of a new method, one that has you go outside the box, rather than just using traditional methods, then consider that one. Dropshipping is an industry that has a lot of competition with it. Finding ways to stand out from the crowd can make a big difference in how successful you will be.

Do Not Underprice the Products

We have talked about this one a little bit, but you have to be careful about the pricing that you have with your products. There are some dropshippers who will try to beat out the competition by lowering the prices of their products by quite a bit. They think this is a surefire way to convince customers to work with them. While this may seem like a good idea, and some customers do like to look for a good deal, it can backfire on you on occasion.

Many customers know the price of other products, or they know how to search online and compare. If they see that the price you are listing at is too low, then they will be wary and assume that they are going to get a substandard product that they won't want, and you won't be able to make many sales in the process.

At the same time, you won't be able to earn as much income in the process either. The lower you make the price, the less profit you are able to make on that item. If you price it too low, the shipping costs and other costs will take up any profit that you make, and it is possible that you would owe money instead of making any money if you aren't careful.

Pick a Product That Makes a Good Profit Margin

There are a lot of dropshipping products that you can choose from when starting out your new business. But you need to make sure that you go with products that are going to earn you a good deal of profit in the process. If you are only going to earn $1 on each product, then it is probably not a good option to go with. You would have to sell thousands of those each month in order to make any profit at all on them.

The higher the profit margin on the item, the better it is going to be for your business. You can sell a good deal of the items, and make a ton more money in the process. Finding products that make at least 45 percent margin after you pay for shipping and taxes, can be great as well. And if you can find products where you can make a profit of $100 or more, that is even better.

How do you make sure that you are finding products that will make you a good amount of profit? First, go through your supplier's pages and decide which products you are the most interested in. Then you can take a look at how much each of those products costs for you to purchase them from the supplier. With that number in mind, go online and see how much other suppliers are charging for that same item.

The last step is important because you want to make sure that your products are priced in a competitive manner. You want to get the most out of the pricing, but you also need to be careful not to price too high compared to the competitors. If you look at the price that the supplier is charging and compare it to the price others are charging for that item, and you see the profit margin is too low, then it is time to move on to a different product. Take your time here and search around until you are able to find the right products that will make you enough money to make the process worth your time.

Find Ways to Bundle Items Together

As a dropshipper, it is your job to find ways that make your business stand out from the others. One way that you can do this is to bundle together some of the items that you are selling. This can be beneficial both for your customer and for you.

Many customers want their shopping experience to be as pleasant and quick as possible. They don't want to spend hours looking for items online that go together or will work together. If you are able to provide them with a bundle of the items they need in one spot, and if you can even provide it with a little bit of a discount, they are more likely to make that purchase.

This method is going to benefit you as well. When you get the customer to purchase the bundle, that means a bigger sale for you. If you are able to find a way to turn it into a subscription service, where the customer will purchase the same bundle or product each month so you can keep earning the same income from it over and over again.

Pick the Right Platform That You Like the Best

We spent some time talking about a lot of different platforms that you can use to start this kind of business. Each one has benefits and negatives that you are going to be faced with, and it is up to you to choose which one seems the best for your needs. Some of the bigger sites, like Amazon, Shopify, and eBay can be nice because they already have a lot of name recognition that goes with them, and you will already find a lot of customers to work with there.

But there are also some benefits that come with working on your own personal website to sell products. You get more choices with the templates that you want to use, you get the benefit of more options with how the website works. And, on the long run, these personal websites often end up being cheaper to use and maintain compared to the other options.

Always Provide the Best Customer Service

Customer service is always important, and it is definitely something that you need to pay attention to when it comes to selling your own dropshipping products. There is going to be a ton of competition out there, and one of the ways that you can make yourself stand out from the crowd is to provide the customers with the best service possible.

There are many different methods that you can choose that will help you to do that. You can make it easy for the customer to email or contact you and ask any questions that they may have. You can bundle your products and services together to make things easier and even cheaper for your customers. In some cases, sending along a little gift, a personalized note, or even some other special offer can help to provide great customer service that they are going to appreciate and will keep them coming back later on.

Order the Product Yourself Before Selling it

This can be a great method to get the same experience that your customer will when they order from you. It is also a good way to ensure that you are picking out the right supplier for your needs. If you have to go through the whole process just like your customers do, then you will see where the issues can be, and you can decide if that supplier is the right one for you or if you need to pick out someone else.

To do this process, simply go to the supplier page and order one or more of their products, the ones that you should like to sell to the customer. Fill in all the information and choose the shipping options that you will provide to your customers. Then sit back and wait.

When the product comes, note how long it took and whether or not that time frame is within the amount the company had promised. Take a look at the packaging and how professional it looks. Open the box and look at the product, determining if it is the right product, if it is made out of high-quality materials, and more. Basically, you want to consider whether or not you would be happy with this product and its speed of delivery if you had actually purchased and wanted this item for yourself.

If you are considering working with a few different suppliers, then it is best to do these steps with each one. If you want to see which company is better than the other when it comes to similar products, order at the same time from them and see what happens. You can compare shipping prices, shipping time, the price of the item, and the quality of the item when it gets to you.

If you find that there are any issues with the company you want to work with, then it may be best to pick out a different supplier. Don't assume that it is just a one-time thing that happened. You are the face of the business, and if a supplier isn't able to provide a good service and impress your customers, then you are going to be the one who is blamed.

If there are any problems, consider working with someone else to ensure you give the best customer experience to anyone who purchases from you.

Starting your dropshipping business can be an exciting time. You have to figure out which products you would like to sell, which supplier is the best one to work with, and make sure that you are pricing and marketing the items so your customers are able to find them. When you are ready to get started with this new business model, make sure to check out these tips to make it a little bit easier to work with.

Conclusion

Thanks for making it through to the end of *Dropshipping E-commerce Business Model 2019*. Let's hope it was informative and able to provide you with all of the tools you need to achieve your goals whatever they may be.

The next step is to use the steps that we talked about in this guidebook in order to help you get started with your own dropshipping business today. There are a lot of different ways to make money in our modern world. Some require a lot of time and effort though, and most of them are not going to provide you with a reasonable amount of money for the time and effort that you put into it in the first place. But when you get started with dropshipping, you will find that things can be different. You will truly run your own business without having to put a pile of money down and without having to hold inventory. A dropshipping business can easily have hundreds of products and you never have to touch a single one in the process. And with this business model, you can choose how big or small your business is at any given time.

This guidebook takes some time to look at the process of dropshipping and what it entails. We look at the basics of dropshipping as well as some of its advantages and disadvantages to getting started with it. We then moved on to some of the basics of getting your own business up and running, how to pick out a good supplier and good products, and how to provide good customer service each and every time.

From there, we moved on to some of the different platforms that you can use to help make that business grow. We looked at Shopify, Amazon, eBay, and even using your own personal website, and the reasons that you would choose to work with each one.

To finish off, we spent some time talking about how you can use social media to enhance your business and spread the word, how affiliate marketing can help you to see more with your business, and how to use Amazon FBA to bring it all together. There are so many ways that you can promote and work on your own business, and this guidebook will take a look at how you can use all of them together to get the most out of your business.

There may be a lot of different online businesses out there, but most of them are going to cost a lot of time and money and inventory just to get your foot in the door. Dropshipping is different. It is available for anyone who is looking to get started with their own business but who wants to be able to limit the amount of risk that they are dealing with for their own online business. When you are ready to get started in dropshipping, make sure to check out this guidebook to help you out!

www.ingramcontent.com/pod-product-compliance
Lightning Source LLC
LaVergne TN
LVHW050208101025
823201LV00003B/10